GROWING UP ON A FARM

LIFE ON THE FARM

Lynn M. Stone

Rourke Publishing LLC
Vero Beach, Florida 32964

www.rourkepublishing.com

PHOTO CREDITS:
All photos © Lynn M. Stone

EDITORIAL SERVICES:
Pamela Schroeder

Library of Congress Cataloging-in-Publication Data

Stone, Lynn M.
    Growing up on a farm / Lynn M. Stone
      p. cm. — (Life on the farm)
    ISBN 1-58952-095-5
     1. Farm life—North America—Juvenile literature. [1. Farm life.] I.
    Title

S519 .S77 2001
630'.973—dc21   2001031670

Printed in the USA

TABLE OF CONTENTS

GROWING UP ON A FARM

Not many people grow up on a family farm in North America anymore. There are fewer and fewer family farms every year. But for some lucky boys and girls, a family farm is home.

Some kids can still call a family farm home.

Most kids grow up in cities or **suburbs**. Growing up on a farm is different. Farms are in rural places "out in the country." Farms are away from busy streets and long rows of buildings.

Farms are surrounded by fields, woods, and creeks. Farm friends often live miles apart. The only way to school is on a school bus.

Most farm kids grow up in rural areas, away from cities and suburbs.

FARM CHORES

Everyone on the farm helps with **chores**. Farm families work together. Children help feed and water animals. They may also clean pens and gather eggs. Older children may help milk cows and drive tractors. Sometimes a herd of cows needs to be rounded up and chased home.

It's a chore when Thanksgiving dinner runs away and has to be caught!

In summer and fall there are garden chores. Berries need to be picked. Corn must be **husked**. Carrots have to be pulled up and washed.

Often baby farm animals need to be bottle fed. Brush needs to be cut. Rocks need to be moved. Trees need trimming. Sometimes firewood needs to be cut and stacked.

Girls fill the feeder for their barred rock chickens.

This girl's 4H Club project is to raise and show a Guernsey calf.

Cattle and kids use farm ponds for different reasons!

FARM FUN

Growing up on a farm isn't all work. Farm kids explore woods and fields. They fish and swim in nearby ponds and rivers.

If they want to, they learn to hunt deer and ducks. They gather maple sap, black walnuts, and Indian arrowheads. Many join the **4H Club** and show their projects at fairs.

Young maple sap collectors share the sweet-tasting sap with work horses.

LIFE ON THE FARM

Farm kids see different things than city kids do. They hear different sounds and smell different scents. Away from city lights, farm kids see a darker sky and brighter stars. Farm kids see animals being born and growing up. Sometimes they see animals die.

Farm kids growing up can watch—and help—animals on the farm grow up.

Farm children see nature at work in many ways. They watch seeds disappear under soil. Then they see stems and flowers and fruit. They see how sunlight and rain turn brown fields into green ones.

Kids on farms hear magical sounds. They hear the spring trilling of toads. They hear the cheery whistles of birds.

Farm kids watch spring pastures turn into cushions of green grass.

Nights are filled with country "music". A cow moos. A locust hums. A frog croaks from a pond edge. A **whip-poor-will** in the woods whistles its name—*whip-poor-will!* An owl answers with a hoot. And morning arrives with a rooster's wakeup call.

When clouds gather, farm kids smell the rain. They smell fresh-cut hay and apple blossoms. They smell sweet maple **sap** steam and evergreens.

A rooster crows from atop an old milk can.

Farmers pass on many skills to their children. Farm kids learn how to fix just about anything that's broken. It doesn't matter whether it's a fence, tractor, or tire.

They learn how to till, plant, and harvest. They learn how to keep record books, run a computer, and call a cow. They become part **mechanic** and part **scientist**. They become part business person and part animal doctor. And some become farmers.

GLOSSARY

chore (CHOR) — a job, especially a farm job

4H Club (FOR AYCH KLUB) — a hands-on club for young people, built around the importance of a person's hands, heart, health, and head

husked (HUSKT) — to have had the paper-like husks covering ears of corn removed

mechanic (meh KAN ik) — a person who fixes machines

sap (SAP) — the clear, watery liquid made by maple trees to carry the trees' food to branches and leaves

scientist (SY en tist) — a person who studies a science such as biology or ecology

suburb (SUB urb) — a smaller town or city nearby to a much larger one

whip-poor-will (HWIP er wil) — a brownish bird of eastern North America that calls loudly from woodlands at night, seeming to whistle its name

INDEX

Further Reading

Avi. *The Barn*. William Morrow, 1996
Yolen, Jane. *Raising Yoder's Barn*. Little, Brown, 1998

Websites To Visit

www.fourhcouncil.edu

About The Author

Lynn Stone is the author of more than 400 children's books. He is a talented natural history photographer as well. Lynn, a former teacher, travels worldwide to photograph wildlife in its natural habitat.